THE DOONESBURY CHRONICLES

Doonesbury Books in Holt Paperback Editions

THE DOONESBURY CHRONICLES

G. B. Trudeau

With an Introduction by Garry Wills

Holt, Rinehart and Winston/New York

25 24 23 22 21 20 19 18 17

ISBN 0-03-015256-9

You could be laughing at me,
You've got the right.
But you go on smiling...
—Jackson Browne

Introduction by Garry Wills

Almost every one of us so-called adult male Americans is a jock manqué. We only decided to be above all that the time when it dawned on us we were just not good enough for the pros—or even for the midget team. (My own basketball was played on a humiliatingly submidget team called "The Mosquitos.") For a while, there was a consolation prize. Perhaps stardom was out of reach; but one might still become the obviously next-best-thing, a sports *announcer*. In fact, we had already been that in all our day-dreaming of stardom. What good is it to knock out a ghostly home run, or dunk a phantom basketball, if the world does not hear of it and shout approval? So watch boys dribbling on a downtown asphalt court or cuffing balls across a sandlot—you will, in time, trace an odd antiphonal pattern of sportscasters "announcing" each boy's game. "Here comes Denny the Dunk up the court, making fantastic moves," Denny reports to the tiered thousands of invisible Denny-fans.

And Lenny, covering him, has his own announcer: "But Slick Lenny has him all sewed up—and almost steals the ball! What hands!" Almost every boy who ever dabbled in sports has spent hours being three things all at once—performer, announcer, and fan. It is one of the basic exercises in that shared human trait of watching, judging, and approving (or groaning at) one's own activity. Chesterton once said that we are the only laboratory specimens that study themselves through a microscope that *is* ourselves.

In 1968 the Yale *Daily News* featured a cartoon strip by an undergraduate named Garry Trudeau. The Yale football team's star quarterback at the time was Brian Dowling, and one way to deflate the superstar back to the general level of us duffers and misfits was to imagine him still doing the internal patter of adulation long after he had acquired a real announcer to celebrate his feats. So there goes big Number Ten, "B.D.," into the huddle—he calls the play as if he were announcing it during the execution: "I fade back to our own five-yard line. Waiting until at least three men are upon me, balancing on one foot, I throw an underhand ninety-five-yard spiral, which I'll run down and catch on the goal line."

But it is even more satisfying to imagine the great B.D. off the field, announcing other kinds of games that all men play. Here he is at a college mixer, beginning to socialize: "While he coolly sips on his ginger ale, the young college quarterback awaits the rush which will undoubtedly come when word gets out that he is here at Briarcliff . . . ." And, just in case they don't recognize him, B.D. is still wearing his football helmet. (Later, of course, B.D. the all-American jock will go to Vietnam and wear that same helmet instead of the military kind—the white Yale helmet even gets autographed by Bob Hope after one of his Christmas shows.)

If it is fun to dream of a successful jock still dreaming of becoming a successful jock, it is even better to watch B.D.'s klutzy roommate, Mike Doonesbury, "announcing" his miserable performances: "Mike 'the Mix,' inexperienced but eager freshman, still looks around for his first score of the evening"—only to be addressed finally as "you gross, skinny frosh." Always, of course, Trudeau's characters give themselves their own sports nicknames, which tend to become ludicrous in other people's mouths. Doonesbury cheers himself on as "Mike the Mix" and "Mike the Man." Mark Slackmeyer, campus radical, comes before us to seize the university president's home: "With discontent in the air, the SDS has staged a rally in front of the president's house, led by 'Megaphone' Mark." Unfortunately for the Megaphone, others reduce him to scale by using the silly diminutive "Megs." You can't win if you're a Trudeau character.

Even the president of Yale, Kingman Brewster, plays sports announcer to his own performance in the campus wars: "It's more kudos for Yale's Youthful President as he starts out on his morning walk through the colleges to reduce tension." But while he preens himself abroad, Slackmeyer has seized his home.

Jim Andrews, of the Universal Press Syndicate, found Trudeau's strip in the *Daily News* and asked to syndicate it commercially. He was repaid, later in their friendship, by entering the strip as an oil magnate during the 1974 gasoline shortage. At first Trudeau just slightly recast his old situations to fit every campus and the family newspapers: The "Y" got scrubbed off B.D.'s helmet, naked girls in the dorms got their clothes put back on, and swear words disappeared. But Trudeau's world opened up when he got into the realm of politics. Despite Megaphone Mark's rallies, and Mike's inept drags on a marijuana joint, there had been only one strip of real political satire in the Yale days—when B.D. so cowed and abused his replacement in a huddle that the rest of the team called the underdog "Hubert."

All that changed in the extraordinarily successful commercial strips from which this book is assembled: B.D. went to war, and Mike started tutoring in the ghetto, and Joanie Caucus ran away from her husband and children to be liberated. Mark even dragged Mike off to a peace march in Washington, where Mike argued with Joe Alsop while Mark called on Vice-President Humphrey (heard still trying to spell his name over the phone to President Nixon).

Yet the world that Trudeau entered remained close to his basic insight. Send B.D. to Vietnam, where he gets captured, and his captor will introduce himself to an inaudible ringside cheer: "Who ain't heard of Phred the Terrorist?" Phred, it turns out, is just joining the family business—his father pressured him into the firm. Zonker Harris, the flowery freak-out who tends Walden Puddle, goes to Vietnam to cover B.D.'s exploits in sportscasts from the front. The coffee-house priest introduces himself in the third person, and with reference to his clips: "The fighting young priest who can talk to the young . . . Birmingham, Selma, Chicago '68." A ghetto tour is conducted as if for television. Jeb Magruder's penitence becomes an "In Concert" traveling show. Everything is "covered" as a sports event.

During the Senate Watergate hearings, Megaphone Mark took a job as a disc jockey and became "Marvelous Mark," playing Watergate profiles as personal-request numbers: "Okay! Profile on John Dean III going out to Joey with hugs from Donna!" When Trudeau had Mark conclude his judicious profile on John Mitchell by doing an ecstatic jig to cries of "Guilty, guilty, guilty!" the Washington *Post* killed the strip and editorialized: "We cannot have one standard for the news pages and another for the comics." I agree. How can the rest of us journalists ever live up to Trudeau's standards?

The sportscaster technique even served Trudeau in the least likely connection—his affectionate portrait of the "libber" Joanie Caucus. Billie Jean King helped, of course. Ms. Caucus and women's sports arrived simultaneously in the day-care center: "We can't *all* wear tennis dresses with blue sequins. Basically, it's just not possible. Anyway, I'm thinking of changing to Margaret Mead." That last sentence shows us why the self-announcing trait of Trudeau's characters is not limited to males or to jocks. Joanie's day-care children are only liberated by taking on role-models—"B.J." King, or Ms. Mead, or Joanie herself. And even Joanie can only break the mold of what she is "supposed" to be by taking up a publicly defined role—"women's libber," a type delivered to her in the newspapers. She is testing her "game" against Betty Friedan's, as surely as the sandlot kid is re-enacting a Ted Williams performance.

Trudeau's way of making characters deliver a running commentary on their own acts, a commentary cast in the third person, opens up that inner space in which personality can grow. We think too often of "playing a role" as something artificial, at odds with reality. But we are all role-players, to our roots. We become by pretending. We feign humanity. We must "play" child before we get a chance to "play" adult—and in both cases we are quietly watching and indulgently grading (even while fearing or resenting) our own performance. The process of growth is in large part a willingness to risk new roles—something Joanie perfectly exemplifies in her breakout. She runs away on Mark's motorbike long after she should have "settled down" in her one role as wife-mother. B.D. kids Mike when the cyclists arrive back at the commune with Joanie: "Little of the ol' Mrs. Robinson, eh, Mikey?" But Joanie, getting on toward Mrs. Robinson's age, is more like the kids in *The Graduate*. Except that her breakout is both more difficult and more realistic—she is rushing off to find a job, not to escape one. In fact, eventually she will be "A Graduate"—a new role for her—if Berkeley's law school survives her incursion. And meanwhile she teaches not only her day-care charges, but her young friends in the commune as well.

Humor is always complex and precarious—the Real's nervous *j'accuse* hurled at the Ideal, in the name of the Ideal. That is why the humor that ultimately fails is the kind that does not take itself seriously enough—without the risk, there is no joke. And a humor that has Trudeau's starting point makes its own complexity the point. Mike at the mixer *is* what he bills himself as: "Inexperienced but eager freshman" looking around for his first score. But that hardly makes him "Mike the Mix." Still, he must try to be Mike the Mix in order to stand his ground at all, to keep from running away. We all only pretend to be heroes—even our heroes. (That is what B.D. is all about.)

Trudeau's characters are watching each other watch themselves, just like the rest of us. We travel toward ourselves by detours only. We grow not so much by addition as by division—and multiplication. The more "things" we are, the more roles we have tried, the more we become a unique and united self. The "simple" man is less than a man, and much of a corpse. The complex man is an army on the move. That is why Trudeau's kind of talking-to-oneself is the only way, finally, to communicate with others.

Trudeau's approach has a very practical effect on his strip. Since his characters are caught in the process of defining themselves over-against some public role, they have no trouble moving out, anywhere, into the world. Mark can as easily talk to Hubert Humphrey as to Brian Dowling or to "King" Brewster. That is not as common an ability as one might think in today's "funnies," which have by and large tended a small "lyrical" garden and an inner world. "Peanuts" is as good an example as any: Its world is a playground uncontaminated by adults, or even by the clothes, furniture, or reminders of adults. The strip says that we are all children; there are no adults. That view has just enough truth in it to get by, but the strip does so by a drastic narrowing. The fantasy-for-its-own-sake ends up logically in a dog's dream of being a German air-ace. This is not role-playing as a way of trying on a world to see if it fits, but as a way of escaping the world. Happiness is a toy puppy's nose. Much the same thing can be said of Broom Hilda's blasted heath, or Pogo's later (desiccating) swamp. Al Capp kept his strip alive so long because Abner could leave Dogpatch and go to Washington, or to Lower Slobbovia. When Walt Kelly dragged Joe McCarthy and Spiro Agnew into the swamp, that upset its ecology forever. The more interesting characters, like Miz Mam'selle Hepzibah and Porky Pine, began to lose their particular reality.

The natural terminus of this shrinking "inner world" of comedy is the solipsism of Jules Feiffer's characters, who pursue themselves expressionlessly through panel after panel and crumble when they catch themselves. Trudeau has obviously learned from Feiffer; he uses repeated panels with little or no visual change to indicate thought processes going on *behind* a façade. But Feiffer's characters are stranded in a desert of themselves, while Trudeau's people interact. Indeed, it is when he is superficially most like Feiffer that the difference becomes clearest.

Richard Nixon is a voice coming out of the TV set, that just sits there for panel after panel. Then, at the end, even klutzy Mike Doonesbury's head drops in embarrassment for the overreacher's last mendacity. The "Nixon" portrayed here—or, rather, studiously left unportrayed—is not the historian's Nixon, or the journalist's. He is the Nixon whose voice enters Walden Puddle's commune and makes its residents react. He is the Nixon B.D. praises when others wonder how the man kept a silly war going so long: "The President is a lot smarter than you think."

So Trudeau, despite his sketchy and Feifferesque economy of drawing, has brought narrative back to the *funny* strips (as opposed to inked-in soap operas), where it has been missing since the great days of Capp's schmoos and kygmies. B.D.'s capture by Phred gave Trudeau a way to arch a single story over several weeks while keeping each segment funny. And we have to keep reminding ourselves of the truly astonishing achievement this represents—that he made us laugh at the Vietnam war during its most corrosive stages. Trudeau's Vietnam was, to the late sixties, what Capp's Slobbovia was to the Cold-War forties.

Yet the war strips in Vietnam were not the toughest challenge Trudeau set for himself. For that prize I would nominate the tour de force of Phred's visit to Washington, accompanied by three hundred refugees disguised as Coca-Cola (*they're* the real thing). You have to remember the story (a sign of the characters' strength): Phred, to keep the sports-star analogy alive, was up for renewal of his terrorist contract; but he was asking too much—his mother wanted a fresh motorbike for her *plastiqueuse* getaways. So Phred gets traded to another team (the Pathet Lao). After tiring of the scenery in Laos (mainly refugees as far as the eye can see), he took a tourist flight to beautiful Cambodia, where most of the briefly remaining scenery was also refugees. He asked an oriental Grant Wood couple (complete with pitchfork) if their museum was destroyed in the secret Cambodian bombings:

"*Secret* bombings? . . . I remarked on them. I said, 'Look, Martha, here come the bombs.'"

"It's true, he did."

That set up the situation. Then Trudeau launched four weeks of strips that brought homeless refugees to Washington as congressional witnesses. (They fly in on a plane returning empty Coke bottles to keep a ruined Cambodia beautiful.) Hunger and tragedy yield a weird music of laughter. The hearings, needless to say by now, get "announced" as a quiz show: Who can identify a phantom jet while being bombed by it? What *prizes* for the witnesses? Mike watches the hearings at home. Though he is B.D.'s old roommate, he has not (yet) met Phred. It is a large world Trudeau has taken to roaming in; and only we, the readers, are let into all parts of it.

It is surprising that politics freed Trudeau for these wanderings. The political animals that entered Okefenokee contaminated it, and the later humor of "Li'l Abner" crumpled under a kind of political hatred. Capp's Joanie Phoney was not only less fair than Joanie Caucus, from a political point of view, she was just less funny. Ms. Caucus is not an anti-Phoney. The reason is, again, Trudeau's creative interplay of the self against its roles. Though the satire has bite, it remains surprisingly kindly. There are no really hateful characters in the strip—not even the pilots who casually erase entire countries under their wing-tips while discussing a Knicks game. Mark, the radical, is not hated—and neither are the hard hats who beat him up. Some might consider Phred the acid test—what other artist could make a terrorist amiable? Not even the Watergate criminals were treated with unbridled bitterness. Not even Nixon, who was presented as a kind of Dagwood under his various imperial roles; all the evil demands he made upon himself and could not, mercifully, meet. The most moving cartoon on the President's resignation showed the demolition of a brick wall that grew up around the White House in earlier strips. It seemed more like the freeing of a prisoner than the storming of a bastille.

Over and over Trudeau affects a neat, almost surgical division between indignation and malice. Usually only sanctity can make such hairline incisions; but comedy, too, is a thing of rigor and discipline, a kind of secular asceticism (ask the best of them, Mark Twain). Trudeau's characters fail and bumble themselves into our affection. It is one thing to laugh at a klutz; it is another thing entirely to laugh at a man who is obviously mocking himself for being a klutz. He has co-opted us, this Doonesbury. We laugh with him, in a camaraderie of klutziness. "Mike the Man" is silly. But ridicule only deflates him to "Mike, a Man"—and there is no higher earthly title. Trudeau always sees a person *under* the roles, struggling with them. His wisdom mocks forgivingly, and each target of his ridicule is haloed with laughter's benediction.

Author's Preface:

Four years four months gone by, and I find myself ready to embark on what is shaping up to be an arduous fact-finding mission to Pago Pago, which is, at least this year, the seat of government in American Samoa. Yes, it has come to that. In the event that for one reason or another I don't survive the crossing of the international date line, I must make my peace and leave behind these cryptic notes, with the hope that they will ultimately find their way into the comprehensive retrospective now in the making.

I have just finished reading an astonishingly well-reasoned critique of "Doonesbury," written and sent to me by Alice, age eight, president of a Tallahassee chapter of the Sunshine and Smiles John Denver Fan Club. The letter is filled with angry words for me, for I have slighted her idol in some recent strips, and, as I have learned this past month, hell hath no fury like that of a fan of John Denver scorned. Nonetheless, for all its excesses, the letter seems to me particularly forthright, written with an urgency and directness that invariably characterize the communications of the very young. Walt Kelly, creator of "Pogo," used to believe that cartoonists should be attended at all times by staffs of small, insouciant children in whose wisdom and vision he correctly placed absolute faith. To see through the essentially egalitarian eyes of a child, where nothing escapes notice and everything starts out with an equal importance, is to celebrate the boundless, shimmering diversity of everyday experience. The young seem to reach out to grasp *all* of life's perceptual confetti: colors and cues, sights and sounds, notions of every sort are permitted wondrous entry. Nothing is ignored and nothing is wasted. With wobbly logic and earnest assumptions, children are free to order their priorities more or less randomly; only later are they taught that the blackboard is more important than the wall that frames it.

The rest of us can only envy from afar this tumbled but guileless universe. As the naturalist Annie Dilliard lamented, "I would like to know grasses and sedges—and *care*. Then my least journey into the world would be a series of happy recognitions." And happy recognitions, no matter how seemingly common, are the stuff from which the dreams and fantasies of children are conjured. Nothing else is required. In the quintessential cartoon fantasy of Slumberland in Winsor McCay's "Little Nemo," a small boy dropped off to sleep and the tiniest objects of his day were transformed into the wondrous vehicles of his nights. In his dreams, Nemo floated on a milkweed seed, toppled from a colossal mushroom, and was whisked away in an ivory coach drawn by cream-colored rabbits. The scale of the objects corresponded to the importance that the boy attached to them—hence, giant raspberries and miniature furniture. Through it all, the value of

Slumberland established itself through its contribution to the child's experience, and when the excitement of the vision deposited him, as it always did, in a jumble of sheets on the hardwood floor beside his bed, it was only the artist's implicit assurance that Nemo would have other dreams to explore that kept away the disappointment.

A flight of fantasy, whether in dream or daydream, is no mere sleight of mind. But only children will accept it as being equally as profound as the arbitrary state of awareness we are taught to regard as reality, and hence, only they are nurtured by it. Later, of course, many of us comprehend our self-imposed poverty and try to double back, but the bread crumbs are always missing and our failures are immense. A true belief in the validity of nonordinary reality—with all that it can teach us—seems beyond the capabilities of every practicing adult, with the possible exception of Federico Fellini.

Perhaps this sad state of affairs helps explain the indispensable function of the cartoonist in society. When he's doing his job, he provides us with the means to look back into ourselves; he's the benign conduit between our self-serious façades and those pockets of vulnerability buried deep within. The challenges he negotiates are considerable: to create a compelling fantasy—whether Slumberland or Okefenokee—and to invite the reader to involve himself in a new reality set up as a sustained metaphor for his own; to let the small meannesses and foolishnesses of life face each other in distortion, stretched, juggled, and juxtaposed, but always lit with laughter to ease the pain of self-recognition; to seek out the vignette that speaks much to the lives of many; to distill and refine language so as to epitomize, and to look everywhere for simple meanings—even in the grasses and sedges. These are the purposes of the precious few in this business who have really meant something to their readers; the purposes of artists who had the capability of endowing a given strip with such exquisite flow of allusion that one almost expected it to lift like a decal and float off the page.

As many of the cartoons in this collection amply demonstrate, there are myriad places to go wrong. In what is unavoidably a chronicle of one's own personal maturation, self-indulgence and contrivance abound. And in the pursuit of tomfoolery the desire to join battle sometimes overwhelms. Yet, in more thoughtful moments, I have tried to observe Kelly's famous advice of almost twenty years ago: "There is no need to sally forth, for it remains true that those things which make us human are, curiously enough, always close at hand. Resolve, then, that on this very ground, with small flags waving, and tiny blasts of tinny trumpets, we have met the enemy, and not only may he be ours, he may be us."

Garry Trudeau
New Haven, Connecticut
February 26, 1975

I/High Tides and Greener Grass

It wasn't just Mark Slackmeyer on a proletariat lark, taking a hard-hat job over summer vacation—*everybody* was just dying to establish a dialogue. If you were a college professor, it might help to bring in for your class an actual Black Panther, or offer a course in Consciousness 10-A. Even better if you were a fighting young priest who could talk to the young. Still, communications could be requited, or unrequited, on more fundamental planes: Doonesbury working on his timing at fraternity mixers, Mark's father trying to tune in on his son via "Mod Squad," and B.D. turning from the frustrations of the huddle to the invigorating, simpler pleasures of combat training. Everything, if not everyone, seemed poised.

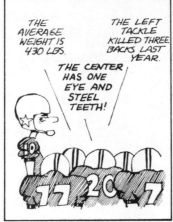

DEAR, I THINK IT'S ABOUT TIME YOU GOT DOWN TO BRASS TACKS AND FOUND A JOB.

YOU CAN'T SPEND YOUR WHOLE LIFE DRINKING BEER IN FRONT OF A T.V. SET.

WHAT ABOUT B.D.? DO YOU WANT YOUR ONLY SON TO THINK THAT HIS FATHER IS A QUITTER AND A LOSER?

FORTUNATELY, I'M TOO DRUNK TO ANSWER THAT QUESTION.

Dear Mr. President; I am writing in protest of my father being laid off at work. He only stays alive by being a janitor nights.

Last spring you said there is just as much dignity in being a janitor as in being President of the United States.

Right.

SOMETIMES A MAN HAS TO RESORT TO SARCASM..

MARIA, A RASH OF NEW BILLS CAME IN TODAY. $650. WORTH!

OH, DEAR, HOW COULD THINGS GET ANY WORSE FOR US?

GOOD AFTERNOON. I'M HERE TO RECLAIM YOUR TELEVISION.

MARIA, REFRESH MY MEMORY..

WHY EXACTLY DID WE LEAVE POLAND?

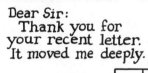

Dear Sir:
Thank you for your recent letter. It moved me deeply.

As President of the United States, I find I usually don't have time to personally answer all my mail.

But your letter conveyed to me a personal problem that I don't hear too much about.

I was greatly saddened to hear that your _father_ was laid off from his job at _the aircraft factory_.

II/The Sounds of Falling Dominoes

There was—had been, would be—a war. "To the 'Nam," B.D. called to his MATS pilot, and indeed there was a certain piquancy to life at Firebase Bundy, though it hardly prepared one for the likes of a Vietcong terrorist named Phred. On the home front a farmer could warble ". . . sweet land of subsidy," and the more callow slackards could huddle in communes. Some, like Zonker, could fall in love with a wheat patch. But the country out there, however schizophrenic, was too big to be ignored, at least so Mike and Mark must have reasoned before setting out on a transcontinental fact-finding motorcycle tour, an odyssey that netted them one runaway housewife. And if Joanie Caucus could turn her life around, so could . . . Zonker get a job as a mailman, the Reverend Scot Sloan go dating, and hard-headed B.D. see what the war was all about in stunned reunion with his pal the terrorist. Lines of sight were adjusting.

SIGH

Z-Z-Z

SLEEP ON, CHARLIE. YOU MAY BE LOST, BUT AT LEAST YOU'RE IN THE RIGHT COUNTRY.

ME, I'M THOUSANDS OF MILES FROM HOME, HUNGRY, TIRED, DISGRACED AND HUMILIATED. HOW COULD THINGS POSSIBLY GET ANY WORSE FOR ME?

Dear John...

SIGH... I SURE AM HUNGRY.. WHAT I'D GIVE FOR A BOWL OF RICE..

...ESPECIALLY MY MOTHER'S RICE! BOY, CAN SHE WHIP UP A MEAN BOWL OF RICE... YOU KNOW, I BET SHE'S WORRIED SICK ABOUT ME. I'VE NEVER LEFT HER ALONE THIS LONG..

AMAZING..

..I DIDN'T KNOW COMMIES HAD MOTHERS.

B.D., I KNOW HOW HARD IT MUST BE FOR YOU TO ACCEPT ME, WHAT WITH OUR DIFFERENT BACKGROUNDS AND ALL. I REALIZE HOW YOU FEEL..

YOU KNOW, I EVEN KNOW WHAT YOU'D LIKE TO CALL ME.. BUT YOU HAVEN'T SAID IT, ON ACCOUNT OF OUR JOINT STRUGGLE FOR SURVIVAL. BUT I WOULDN'T MIND REALLY.. GO AHEAD AND SAY IT.. O.K.

YOU LOUSY COMMIE GOOK!

THERE NOW, DON'T YOU FEEL BETTER? YES, I NEEDED THAT..

WHAT EXACTLY ARE WE LOOKING FOR, PHRED? A CACHE OF SUPPLIES MY MEN HID IN THIS AREA.

HEY, HERE IT IS! IT'S A BOX WE STOLE FROM THE U.S. SUPPLY DEPOT LAST MONTH.. WHAT?

WHAT'S IN IT? DON'T KNOW. WE WERE DISCOVERED AND HAD TO LEAVE IT BEHIND...

BEER!

"SCHLITZ"?

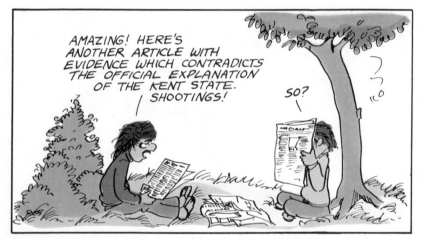

WELL, THERE IT IS, PEOPLE! OUR NEW HOME!

AIN'T IT DANDY? A BIG OL' COUNTRY HOUSE WITH TWELVE ROOMS, A PORCH, AND FORTY ACRES! PERFECT FOR OUR COMMUNE!

YOU LOOK A LITTLE DISAPPOINTED, BERNIE.

WELL... I GUESS I AM..

I WAS KINDA HOPING FOR A RANCH HOUSE WITH ALUMINUM SIDING.

ME, TOO.

'MORNING, MICHAEL.

AH, GOOD MORNING.

NOT SO FAST, SHORTY. I'M NEXT.

JUST RELAX. SEEN MY SOAP? I CAN'T WASH WITHOUT SOAP.

HEY, HERE IT IS!

HI, FOLKS!

HEY, GIMME MY TOWEL BACK!

YOUR TOWEL?

ANYONE SEEN MY ULTRA BRIGHT?

HURRY UP, WILLYA?

WHY ARE YOU ALL UP AT SIX?

TO AVOID THE LINE AT THE BATHROOM.

WELL, BERNARD, WILL YOU LOOK AT THAT?

A PUDDLE!.. WHAT'S A PUDDLE DOING OUT ON A SUNNY DAY LIKE THIS?

IT MUST BE A SPRING-FED PUDDLE!

IMAGINE! A SMALL BODY OF WATER RIGHT ON OUR OWN PROPERTY!

WELL, OF COURSE! ALL THE GREAT COMMUNES HAVE OVERLOOKED SMALL BODIES OF WATER!

WHAT'LL WE CALL IT?

WALDEN PUDDLE.

MICHAEL, I CAN'T TELL YOU HOW DELIGHTED I WAS TO DISCOVER WALDEN PUDDLE! RIGHT HERE ON OUR OWN PROPERTY!

YOU KNOW, I'LL BET I'M THE FIRST HUMAN-TYPE TO LAY EYES ON THAT PUDDLE! WHAT A PUDDLE! WET AND WILD, AND UNPOLLUTED TO BOOT! MAN, I FELT LIKE MAGELLAN, OR CORTÉS, EVEN.

C'MON ZONKER, A PUDDLE'S A PUDDLE.

WELL, YOU CAN SAY THAT, OF COURSE, BUT I'M SURE OF ONE THING ABOUT WALDEN..

..IT'S NOT YOUR RUN-OF-THE-MILL PUDDLE.

As an early riser walks along the beach, he spots a few bubbles far out to sea..

What can it be breaking the still water of the early morn? A crowd of people quickly forms!

As a lone snorkle rises up from the sea, a mighty hue and cry are heard from the people! "Who is that brave man?" they wonder!

C'est moi, Zonker Cousteau!

What seems to be the problem, ensign?... ...We've spotted something on our radar, Cap'n Zonker!

What?... Up periscope!... ...Why, blow me over! It's a trout! And it's attacking! Torpedo tube one, ensign!

Whoosh! Zip!

Dive, dive!... ...Aye, aye sir!

Prepare to surface, Hans!... Yah, Herr Zonker!

Heil, handsome!

Huh? Hans! Down periscope! Zip!

What was that? I believe today it's a U-boat.

They say it's very pretty in Ohio this time of year..

They say it was a very pretty day exactly two years ago today at Kent State.

Have a nice day, John Mitchell.

MAN, THAT WAS SOME FAST BIKING WE PUT IN. I NEVER THOUGHT WE'D MAKE THE CONVENTION.

ISN'T THIS INCREDIBLE? WE'RE ACTUALLY HERE AT THE REPUBLICAN NATIONAL CONVENTION!!

IT'S AMAZING ALRIGHT!

I WONDER WHO'LL BE NOMINATED.

BEATS ME.

THE DELEGATION FROM UTAH CASTS ALL ITS VOTES FOR RICHARD NIXON!

RAH! YEA! YEA! YEA!

MIKE, THIS SESSION IS GETTING SOMEWHAT TEDIOUS..

YEAH, IT IS RATHER A STUDY IN FOREGONE CONCLUSIONS... LET'S SPLIT.

RAH! YEA! YEA! YEA!

THE DELEGATE FROM WALDEN PUDDLE CASTS HIS VOTE FOR THE LONE RANGER!!

WHAT!?

FAR OUT!

WE SURE WERE SURPRISED TO SEE YOU DOWN ON THE FLOOR, ZONKER, WHAT'RE YOU DOING IN MIAMI?

I CAME DOWN WITH MOM! SHE'S A DELEGATE THIS YEAR..

I DIDN'T KNOW THAT!

SURE! SHE'S PUSHING FOR McCLOSKEY NOW, BUT ON THE FIRST BALLOT, SHE NOMINATED ME!

WHAT? YOU?

I WAS A "FAVORITE SON" CANDIDATE.

WE WANT NIXON! WE WANT NIXON!

WE WANT NIXON!! WE WANT NIXON!!

I WANT McCLOSKEY! I WANT McCLOSKEY!

DO YOU HEAR ME?! McCLOSKEY!

MOM'S A VERY SCRAPPY DELEGATE.

WELL, WE'VE GOT TO GET BACK ON THE ROAD, ZONKER.

I SURE HATE TO GO BEFORE ALL THE DELEGATES ACTUALLY LEAVE. SOMETHING IMPORTANT MIGHT HAPPEN AND I'LL MISS IT.

MR. CHAIRMAN, THE DELEGATION FROM RHODE ISLAND REQUESTS PERMISSION TO SEND OUT FOR SOME PIZZA!

I'M OFF.

TAKE CARE.

ZONKER! A POSTCARD FROM MIAMI HAS ARRIVED FOR YOU!

FOR ME? O, HAPPY DAY!

"DEAR ZONKER, I MUST SAY, OL' BOY, YOU CUT A FINE FIGURE AT THE CONVENTION. YOUR PRESENCE WAS A REAL ADDITION.

"AS HARVEST TIME APPROACHES, I WISH YOU WELL WITH YOUR WHEAT PATCH. GOOD LUCK, KID, YOU'RE A RARE HUMAN BEING."

IT'S FROM ME!

SO THIS IS YOUR FIRST VISIT TO SAN FRANCISCO, EH, PILGRIM?

YUP... SAY, ARE THOSE GIRLS DANCING UP THERE REALLY CO-EDS?

YOUR SIGN OUTSIDE! IT SAID "BEAUTIFUL, EXCITING CO-EDS."

WHAT?

OH,...YEAH! SURE! THEY'RE CO-EDS! SUZIE, THE BLONDE THERE, IS A CUM LAUDE FROM WELLESLEY, AND DORIS IS A PHYSICS MAJOR AT STANFORD, AND TIGER-LIPS, THE ONE WITH THE LEGS, SHE'S MATRICULATING AT YALE THIS FALL.

WHY? YOU A COLLEGE MAN?

HEY, ARE YOU A SIGHT FOR SORE EYES!

HOW NOW?

DO YOU REALIZE I'VE BEEN HERE IN SAN FRANCISCO TWO DAYS, AND YOU'RE THE FIRST STREET PERSON I'VE SEEN?! IMAGINE!

HEY, MAN, YOU GOT ANY ACID ON YOU? DO YOU? SURE, YOU DO!

LET ME HAVE A FEW PUFFS, O.K.?

CHECK!

MA'AM, WE'VE COME ALMOST 400 MILES SINCE YOU STOPPED US. BEFORE WE GO ANY FURTHER, MAYBE YOU BETTER TELL US WHO YOU ARE AND WHERE YOU WANT TO GO...

FAIR ENOUGH, BOYS. MY NAME IS JOANIE CAUCUS AND I'M RUNNING AWAY FROM MY HUSBAND CLINTON! IN BRIEF, I GOT FED UP WITH THE MEANINGLESS ROLES THAT DEFINED MY LIFE.

I WANT TO FIND A NEW TOWN WHERE I CAN START A NEW LIFE.... A PLACE WHERE I CAN LIVE OUT A GRACEFUL REPRIEVAL, A PLACE WHERE I CAN BEGIN ANEW.

CLEVELAND, SAY.

HMM..

MS. CAUCUS—IF YOU DON'T MIND A PERSONAL QUESTION, WHEN DID YOU FIRST START HAVING DIFFICULTIES WITH YOUR HUSBAND CLINTON?

WELL, MIKE, IT'S DIFFICULT TO PINPOINT IT, BUT I GUESS IT MIGHT HAVE BEEN ONE NIGHT LAST SUMMER, WHEN HIS BOWLING BUDDIES CAME TO DINNER...

AT THE END OF THE MEAL, ONE OF HIS FRIENDS COMPLIMENTED ME ON MY FRENCH FRIES. CLINTON LEANED BACK IN HIS CHAIR, AND SAID WITH A BIG, STUPID GRIN, "MY WIFE, I THINK I'LL KEEP HER!"

I BROKE HIS NOSE.

HOME! HOME!

HOME! HELLOOO!

WALDEN

ZONKER! HEEE WACKITY DO, DO, DOO!

-BOING!

HOME? HOME.

LET ME LOOK AT YOU! O.K.

SO THAT'S OUR DEAL— IF YOU HELP WITH THE COMMUNE, YOU CAN STAY UNTIL YOU FIND SOME SORT OF JOB!

MIKE, I CAN'T THANK YOU ENOUGH...

BUT IN ALL FAIRNESS, I MUST WARN YOU— WE HAVE SOME VERY WEIRD PEOPLE IN OUR GROUP.

OH, THAT'S ALRIGHT, DEAR, I...

KABOOM!!

LOOK, THINK IT OVER...

SURPRISE!

HOW'D YOUR DATE WITH REVEREND SLOAN GO, JOANIE?

O.K., I GUESS. I DIDN'T REALLY GET TO KNOW HIM. HE'S AWFULLY SHY AND HE DIDN'T REALLY SAY TOO MUCH..

..BUT THEN I GUESS IT REALLY WASN'T THE RIGHT ATMOSPHERE TO GET TO KNOW SOMEONE REAL WELL.

WHERE'D HE TAKE YOU?

TO VESPERS.

WHAT FUN.

JOANIE? HI. IT IS I, REVEREND SCOT SLOAN. HOW HAVE YOU BEEN?.. GOOD, JUST GRAND.

SAY, JOANIE, I WAS WONDERING IF YOU WOULD LIKE TO ATTEND THE STRING QUARTET RECITAL TOMORROW... WHAT? ...A LONG WALK IN THE PARK INSTEAD?

≡GULP≡

YOU SURE YOU WANT TO DO SOMETHING THAT SECULAR?

HOW DID THE OL' SOIRÉE SHAPE UP LAST NIGHT, REV? HAVE A GOOD TIME WITH MS. CAUCUS?

ZONKER, I DID A TERRIBLE THING LAST NIGHT— AN AWFUL, SEXIST THING!

OH, C'MON, REV. I'M SURE IT WASN'T THAT BAD! WHATJA DO, YOU OL' SCOUNDREL?

I..I... HELD HER HAND..

NO!

AND ME, A MAN OF THE CLOTH!

I KNOW! I KNOW!

I'D LOVE TO GO, SCOT, BUT I JUST DON'T THINK IT'S WORKING OUT FOR US. EVEN THOUGH WE'VE GOTTEN TO KNOW EACH OTHER, YOU STILL ACT LIKE I'M A FRAGILE LITTLE SCHOOL-GIRL.

SCOTTY, I JUST WANT TO BE TREATED LIKE A PERSON, NOT PORCELAIN CHINA! I ADMIRE YOU, YOU KNOW THAT, BUT I THINK WE'VE KIND OF REACHED AN IMPASSE!

DON'T LET HER DO THAT TO YOU, SCOT! SAY SOMETHING TOUGH, BITTER!..

YOUR LOSS, TOOTS!

DEAN'S LIST? INCREDIBLE! YOUR BOY MARK HAS COME A LONG WAY SINCE HIS DAYS ON THE OL' BARRICADES.

YOU BET HE HAS! AND I'VE GOT A FEELING IT'S ONLY A BEGINNING! HE'S GOING TO MAKE THAT DEAN'S LIST AGAIN NEXT TERM!

AND THEN AGAIN! AND THEN GRADUATION WITH PHI BETA KAPPA... AND THEN — DARE I SAY IT?...

LAW SCHOOL?

HEY, WOULDN'T THAT BE SOMETHING?

O.K., DEAR, I'LL PUT YOUR WINTER COAT IN THE MAIL FIRST THING TOMORROW.

OH, MARK, YOUR REPORT CARD CAME YESTERDAY. YOUR FATHER RAN RIGHT OUT AND HAD IT FRAMED. HE'S HANGING IT UP IN HIS STUDY NOW.

MARK, DEAR, WHATEVER OTHER SATISFACTIONS YOU MAY DERIVE FROM THIS SCHOLARLY ACHIEVEMENT, I HOPE YOU KNOW YOU'VE MADE YOUR FATHER VERY, VERY HAPPY.

:SIGH:

I HEARD FROM PHRED TODAY. HE WANTS ME TO SPEND VACATION OVER IN THE 'NAM. I THINK I JUST MIGHT GO...

I KNOW WHAT YOU'RE GONNA SAY: "PINKOS ARE BAD NEWS!" BUT PHRED'S DIFFERENT FROM MOST OF THEM TYPES. HE OFTEN DRINKS BEER, AND HE LIKES CHUCK BERRY RECORDS.

AND WHILE I DETEST HIS POLITICS, YOU GOTTA ADMIRE HIS DEDICATION. HE'S BEEN WORKING FOR THE V.C. FOR A LONG TIME! PHRED'S NO COMMIE-COME-LATELY, YOU KNOW!

UH-HUH.

OR AM I JUST RATIONALIZING?

UH-HUH.

HEY, YOU! ROUNDTRIP LAGUARDIA.

YESSIR.

ANOTHER RUDE COMMUTER! BOY, AM I GETTING SICK OF THEM!

BUSINESSMEN OFF TO MAKE BUSINESS. THEY'RE ALL I EVER SEE-HUNDREDS OF 'EM - ALL GOING OFF TO CHICAGO OR NEW YORK OR BOSTON!

ONE-WAY SAIGON, WITH A CONNECTION TO QUANG-TRI.

'BYE, MOM! BE GOOD NOW!

SHE'S A COURAGEOUS SOUL, PHRED.

SHE CERTAINLY IS. SHE'S PUT IN THOUSANDS OF MILES ON THE ROAD OVER THE YEARS.

AND FOR A REFUGEE, SHE'S PRETTY RESOURCE-FUL. SEE THAT KNAPSACK SHE'S GOT ON? SHE GOT THAT FROM AN ABANDONED FIREBASE.

WHERE'D SHE GET THE MOTORCYCLE?

I'M NOT SURE.

HEY! I THOUGHT THIS HAMLET LOOKED FAMILIAR! I USED TO GO TO SCHOOL HERE!

REALLY?

SURE! THIS WAS MY OLD SCHOOL-HOUSE RIGHT IN FRONT OF US! OVER THERE WAS THE PLAY AREA!

WHAT MEMORIES THIS RUBBLE BRINGS BACK! ARITHMETIC, GEOGRAPHY, CHALK FIGHTS!... THIS WAS MY CLASSROOM RIGHT HERE!

HEY! MY OLD DESK!

MAN, THAT WAS SOME KINDA SHELLING! MUST HAVE BEEN SOME OF YOUR BOYS...

HEY, LOOK, PHRED! THERE'S A GUY OVER THERE WHO LOOKS HURT! MAYBE WE SHOULD GET HELP FOR HIM.

OH, NO NEED TO WORRY ABOUT HIM! HE'S JUST ONE OF MILLIONS OF CIVIL-IANS WHO HAVE BEEN WOUNDED OR KILLED IN THE LAST TEN YEARS!

WHAT'S EATING YOU?

...I'M SORRY... I'VE JUST GOT A BAD HEADACHE...

BLAM!

BOOM!

YOU HEARTLESS AIR PIRATES!

I HOPE YOU CAN LIVE WITH IT! I HOPE YOU CAN LIVE WITH ALL THE DESTRUCTION AND CARNAGE YOU'VE BROUGHT TO MY LITTLE COUNTRY!!

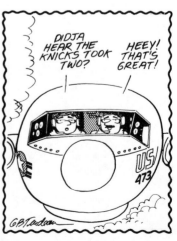

DIDJA HEAR THE KNICKS TOOK TWO?

HEEY! THAT'S GREAT!

US 473

III/A Lasting Piece of the Action

Disengagements become rife, with mixed blessings for the disengaged. Phred, on his own now, finds himself traded to the Pathet Lao, but seeing the ghost of America haunting almost all of Indochina, he is inspired to return the memories by organizing an airlift of homeless Cambodians to Washington, allowing liberal congressmen, and even Georgetown matrons, to adopt their very own refugees. But before patronization comes recrimination—whether at the White House, toiling in the coils of Watergate, on the lecture circuit with a flamboyantly penitent Jeb Magruder, or the more traditional mumblings at the class of '43 reunions. All such turns and pangs are witnessed bucolically by the denizens of Walden Commune, though not without contributions of their own—such as Mark taking to the airwaves as a DJ with Watergate profiles ("Guilty, guilty, guilty!"), and Joanie working wonders at the day-care center in extracting sexism from her scruffy charges.

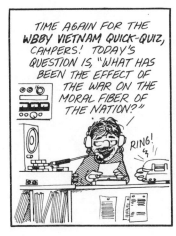

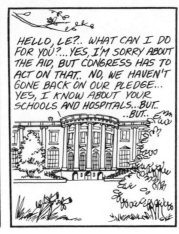

RON, DOES THE PRESIDENT HAVE ANY COMMENT ON THE MOST RECENT DISCLOSURES IN THE WATERGATE CASE!

NO!

WATERGATE! WATERGATE! WHAT IS THE MATTER WITH YOU GUYS?! WHAT IS THIS **SENSELESS** ORGY OF RECRIMINATION WEEK AFTER WEEK?!

I'VE ALREADY SAID ALL THAT I'M GOING TO! SO WHY DON'T YOU STOP WASTING BOTH OUR TIME AND ASK ME QUESTIONS I CAN DEAL WITH?

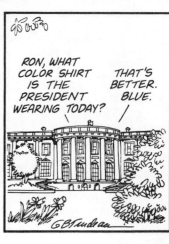

RON, WHAT COLOR SHIRT IS THE PRESIDENT WEARING TODAY?

THAT'S BETTER. BLUE.

MR. PRESIDENT, THE PRESS IS STILL GIVING RON A PRETTY HARD TIME. THERE'S EVEN MORE CLAMORING FOR DETAILS ON WATERGATE.

YES, YES, I KNOW! I TALKED WITH HIM AGAIN THIS AFTERNOON. WE'RE JUST GOING TO HAVE TO KEEP RIDING IT OUT..

BAH! I CAN'T BELIEVE I'M STILL WASTING MY DAYS WORRYING ABOUT THIS THING!

AND ONLY 1337 LEFT, SIR.

OH, SHUT UP!

NICHOLE, HAVE YOU HEARD ABOUT MARK'S NEW SERIES OF PROFILES ON HIS RADIO SHOW?

NO. WHAT'S IT ON?

THE WATERGATE CONSPIRATORS. HE'S WORKED OUT COMPLETE BIOGRAPHIES ON ALL OF THEM.

BOY, I'LL BET THEY'RE JUST **BRUTAL!**

NOT AT ALL. I READ THEM LAST NIGHT. SOME OF THEM ARE QUITE SENSITIVE.

"LOS ANGELES IS A LONELY TOWN TO GROW UP IN, ESPECIALLY IF YOU'RE A SMALL BOY NAMED H.R. HALDEMAN."

HOW'D YOU LIKE MY PROFILE OF HALDEMAN YESTERDAY, B.D.?

I DIDN'T! YOU MADE IT SOUND LIKE HE WAS COMPLETELY UNFIT FOR HIS JOB FROM THE START!

BUT IT'S TRUE! HAVE YOU ANY IDEA WHAT H.R. WAS BEFORE HE BECAME ONE OF THE MOST POWERFUL MEN ALIVE?

SURPRISE ME!

AN ADVERTISING EXECUTIVE! WITH ABSOLUTELY NO EXPERIENCE IN GOVERNMENT!

SO WHAT?! WHAT DOES **THAT** PROVE?!

HOW DO YOU KNOW HE DIDN'T DO A LOT OF READING UP ON HIS OWN?!

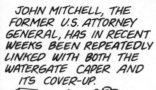

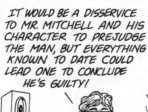

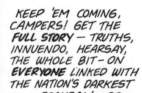

"UPON YOUR EXIT FROM THE **HO CHI MINH** TRAIL, TURN LEFT ONTO THE SCENIC MOUNTAIN PATH WHICH TRAVERSES THE HIGH COUNTRYSIDE."

"IF THE FERRY OVER THE MEANDERING **MEKONG** ISN'T WORKING, YOU MAY HAVE TO GET YOUR FEET WET. BE SURE TO BRING ALONG SOME DRY, LIGHTWEIGHT SUMMER CLOTHES FOR WHEN YOU REACH THE OTHER SIDE."

"A QUICK SCRAMBLE UP THE BEAUTIFUL **DINO-LINO** CLIFF FORMATION AND YOU SHOULD BE ABLE TO SPOT A SMALL LEDGE 80 YARDS ABOVE YOU. A SHORT, SPIRITED HIKE, AND THE TOURIST WILL SOON FIND HIMSELF AT THE TOP."

"WELCOME TO LAOS."

SIR?.. OH, SIR?..

PARDON US, SIR! WE ARE DESTITUTE, HUNGRY REFUGEES ON OUR WAY TO VIENTIANE! TAKE **PITY** ON US!

WE HAVE NOT EATEN IN **DAYS**! COULD NOT SOME OF US SHARE IN THE HOT RICE DINNER YOU HAVE PREPARED FOR YOURSELF?

UM..SURE. HOW MANY ARE THERE OF YOU?

135,000.

"ON YOUR LEFT, YOU SHOULD NOW SEE THE FAMOUS "**JUMPING JARS INN**.." THIS QUAINT LITTLE RESTAURANT WITH ITS SIDEWALK TABLES HAS BEEN A FAVORITE WITH VISITORS FOR YEARS."

"BE SURE TO ASK FOR THE PROPRIETOR, 'LOO': HE'LL BE DELIGHTED TO SERVE YOU ONE OF HIS TASTY, TANGY PUNCHES FOR WHICH HE IS RENOWNED THROUGHOUT THE PROVINCE."

"LOO"?

SORRY, MAN, WE'RE CLOSED.

AW, C'MON, LOO! CAN'T YOU EVEN FIX ME A LIGHT SNACK?

LOOK! I TOLD YOU! I'M **CLOSED**! I'VE BEEN BOMBED OUT OF BUSINESS!

LISTEN TO THIS, LOO: "WHILE THE LAOTIANS ARE A PROUD AND FIERCELY TENACIOUS PEOPLE, THEIR MOST OUT-STANDING CHARACTERISTIC IS **GENEROSITY**!

"WHETHER FOR A FRIEND IN NEED OR A PASSING STRANGER, THE LAOTIANS ARE ALWAYS QUICK ON THE DRAW WHEN IT COMES TO **KINDNESS, COMPASSION**, AND LENDING A **HELPING HAND**!

"FURTHERMORE.".

ALRIGHT ALREADY! I'LL TURN ON THE GRILL!

WELL, HENRY?..

MR. PRESIDENT, I REALIZE THE SITUATION **IS** DETERIORATING OVER THERE, BUT I'M AFRAID ABSOLUTELY **NO ONE** ACCEPTS "PROTECTIVE REACTION" AS A CREDIBLE CONCEPT THESE DAYS.

HMM... WELL, WHAT ABOUT MY OTHER IDEA?

SIR?

"CAMBODIAZATION."

FORGET IT.

WILL THERE BE ANYTHING ELSE THIS MORNING, MR. PRESIDENT?

NO, NO,.. I GUESS NOT, HAIG..

YOU SEEM A LITTLE DEPRESSED THIS MORNING, SIR..

≥ SIGH ≤.. I AM, OLD FRIEND, I AM...

HAIG.. YOU KNOW WHAT I NEED RIGHT NOW? I NEED SOMETHING TO BOOST MY MORALE, TO PICK UP MY SPIRITS...

HOW ABOUT IF I SEND OUT FOR SOME P.O.W.'S, SIR?

WHY... YES! THAT WOULD BE NICE!

WE INTERRUPT THE SENATE WATERGATE HEARINGS TO BRING YOU THIS SPECIAL BULLETIN.

TODAY ON THE PRE-EMPTED SOAP OPERA, "AS THE HOSPITAL TURNS," DR. HARDIN FINALLY DECIDED TO DIVORCE HIS WIFE RACHEL, AFTER FIVE YEARS OF MARRIAGE! A BITTER CUSTODY FIGHT IS EXPECTED.

TO REPEAT: DR. HARDIN IS GETTING A DIVORCE FROM RACHEL! THAT'S A FINAL.

WE NOW RETURN TO OUR REGULARLY SCHEDULED BROADCAST.

LEONARD, AS MY COUNSEL, I THINK IT'S ABOUT TIME YOU TOOK A LOOK AT THESE TRANSCRIPTS OF THE SECRET TAPES...

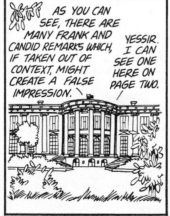

AS YOU CAN SEE, THERE ARE MANY FRANK AND CANDID REMARKS WHICH, IF TAKEN OUT OF CONTEXT, MIGHT CREATE A FALSE IMPRESSION.

YESSIR. I CAN SEE ONE HERE ON PAGE TWO.

WHICH ONE'S THAT?

"WELL, JOHN, HOW'S THE COVER-UP GOING?"

RIGHT! A GOOD EXAMPLE!

YESSIR. IT **COULD** BE MISINTERPRETED.

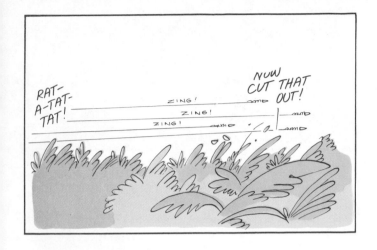

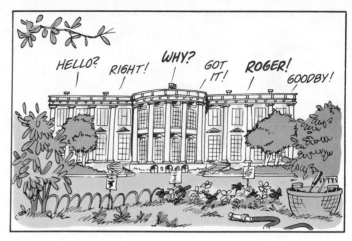

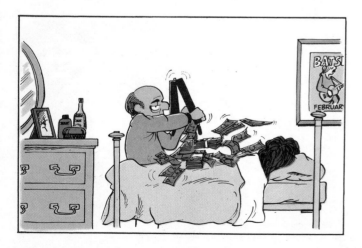

SAY, HOW MUCH LONGER 'TIL VACATION?

SEVEN DAYS, THREE HOURS, AND TWENTY MINUTES.

YOU KNOW, SOMETIMES I KIND OF MISS OL' TED AGNEW. I WONDER WHAT HE'S UP TO THESE DAYS...

SEARCH ME, LADY.

HE'S PROBABLY SPENDING HIS DECEMBER DAYS AT THE PALM SPRINGS HIDEAWAY OF AN AGING BUT CURIOUSLY UNRETIRED CROONER...

HE'S LICKING HIS WOUNDS, AND NO DOUBT STILL FEELS QUITE VICTIMIZED BY... "THE NEW POST-WATERGATE MORALITY"!

"THE NEW POST-WATERGATE MORALITY"... I WONDER WHAT HE MEANT BY THAT... WHAT EXACTLY IS "THE NEW POST-WATERGATE MORALITY"?

I MEAN, I FEEL THE SAME WAY ABOUT BRIBERY AND EXTORTION NOW AS I DID A YEAR AGO!

YEAH, WELL, YOU'RE WEIRD.

NONSENSE! TA, TA, FELLOW CITIZENS!

GOOD EVENING. WELCOME TO *ABC NEWS!*

HARRY'S ON VACATION, AND HOWARD'S ON ASSIGNMENT. FRANK IS ON THE ROAD.

SAM IS OFF THE AIR, TOM IS IN TRANSIT, AND TINA IS OUT TO LUNCH. I'M THE ONLY ONE LEFT HERE. MY NAME IS CARLOS; I WORK UPSTAIRS IN THE STOCK-ROOM.

HERE ARE TONIGHT'S HEADLINES..

BUT CONGRESSMAN, YOU HAVE TO VIEW THE SECRET CAMBODIAN BOMBINGS IN PERSPECTIVE, IN THE PROPER TIME-FRAME!

TIME-FRAME, GENERAL?

YES, SIR.. YOU SEE, THERE WERE DOZENS OF BOMBINGS ON CAMPUSES ALL ACROSS THE COUNTRY..

NATURALLY, THAT KIND OF ATMOSPHERE LED A FEW WELL-INTENTIONED BUT OVERZEALOUS OFFICIALS TO BELIEVE THAT BOMBING WAS AN ACCEPTABLE MEANS OF SOCIAL CHANGE.

OH, *THAT* TIME-FRAME!

YES, SIR.

WHAT IS IT, HAIG?

SIR, IT'S ABOUT THE HOUSE HEARINGS ON THE SECRET CAMBODIAN BOMBINGS...

WE NEED TO KNOW MORE ABOUT THE RAIDS, SIR. THEY SAY NOBODY BUT YOU KNEW ABOUT THEM.

IT'S NOT TRUE! I TOLD EVERYBODY WHO HAD A NEED OR RIGHT TO KNOW!

YES, SIR, BUT WHO? YOU'VE GOT TO BE MORE SPECIFIC.

WELL, LET ME SEE... THE PILOTS, OF COURSE...

YES, GO ON...

JOANIE, I WONDER IF YOU'D BREAK YOUR DATING MORATORIUM AND GO OUT WITH ME TONIGHT..

THANKS, SCOT, BUT I'D REALLY RATHER NOT...

GEE, I THINK YOU'LL REGRET IT, JOANIE. I REALLY DO..

WHAT DO YOU MEAN, SCOT?

WELL, YOU SEE, I JUST HAPPEN TO HAVE TWO TICKETS TO THE JEB MAGRUDER CONCERT..

SCOT! HONEY!

HEE, HEE... AT WHAT POINT IN TIME SHALL I PICK YOU UP?

WELL, LOOK, MICK, JUST LOAD UP THE AMPS, AND I'LL GET TOM TO DO THE REST..

O.K.

CAN I HELP YOU?

YES, I'M FROM THE CAMPUS RADIO, MR. MAGRUDER. I WONDER IF YOU COULD TELL ME WHAT YOUR PLANS ARE..

WELL, I'VE GOT A GIG AT AUBURN NEXT WEEK, THEN THE UNIVERSITY OF ILLINOIS, AND THEN A BENEFIT CONCERT IN L.A..

BENEFIT CONCERT? FOR WHOM?

DUNNO YET... PROBABLY AN EARTHQUAKE FUND OR SOMETHING...

RING! RING! RING! BZZZ! RING! BRRR! RING!

HELLO? YES? JONES HERE. WHAT IS IT? YEAH?

FINE! SEND HIM IN! RIGHT! YESSIR! RIGHT AWAY! VERY GOOD! I'LL GET ON IT! LET ME CHECK..

AAA!!!H... THE PEOPLE'S BUSINESS!

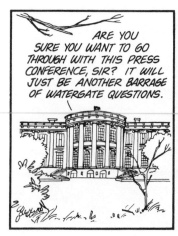

ARE YOU SURE YOU WANT TO GO THROUGH WITH THIS PRESS CONFERENCE, SIR? IT WILL JUST BE ANOTHER BARRAGE OF WATERGATE QUESTIONS.

NONSENSE! THEY'LL WANT TO KNOW ABOUT THE MID-EAST, WHY I HAVE TAKEN THE BOLD AND DECISIVE ACTION OF PUTTING OUR TROOPS ON WORLDWIDE MILITARY ALERT!

BUT SIR, THE TROOPS AREN'T ON A WORLDWIDE MILITARY ALERT.

THEY'RE NOT? BUT.. BUT.. THIS MORNING I GAVE DIRECT ORDERS...

HAIG!

OH, GEE, I'M SORRY, SIR, I FORGOT...

TODAY AT A PRESS CONFERENCE, THE PRESIDENT LASHED OUT AT THE TELEVISION MEDIA FOR WHAT HE CALLED BIASED COVERAGE OF THE WATERGATE AFFAIR.

SAID MR. NIXON, "IN ALL MY YEARS OF POLITICS, NEVER HAVE I SEEN SUCH OUTRAGEOUS, VICIOUS, DISTORTED, AND ERRONEOUS REPORTING!"

HE WENT ON TO CONDEMN TELEVISION COMMENTATORS FOR "THE VINDICTIVE LEERS AND SNEERS DIRECTED AT THE GREAT OFFICE OF THE PRESIDENCY."

MOST REPORTERS PRESENT AGREED THE PRESIDENT WAS BEING HIS USUAL, ASININE SELF.

THIS IS DAN RATHER AT SAN CLEMENTE, A.K.A. "THE WESTERN WHITE HOUSE."

THE SUMMIT TALKS BETWEEN PRESIDENT NIXON AND SOVIET PARTY CHIEF BREZHNEV CONTINUED TODAY AS THE TWO LEADERS SAT OUTSIDE IN THE GARDENS OF THE CALIFORNIA ESTATE.

AT ONE POINT THIS AFTERNOON, MR. BREZHNEV TURNED TO HIS HOST AND INQUIRED WHEREVER DID HE FIND THE FUNDS TO FINANCE AND KEEP UP SUCH A *LOVELY* HOME!

IT WAS CONSIDERED BY MANY TO BE A LOW POINT IN THE TALKS.

GOOD EVENING. PRESIDENT NIXON AND SOVIET CHIEF BREZHNEV ENGAGED IN ANOTHER ROUND OF VIGOROUS TALKS TODAY.

IT WAS LATER ANNOUNCED THAT THEY HAD REACHED AGREEMENT ON A NEW BILATERAL PENAL-REFORM PROGRAM, WITH A MUTUAL EXCHANGE OF PRISONERS.

UNDER THE NEW ACCORD, THE U.S. WILL SEND THE SOVIETS THREE BLACK MILITANTS, FOUR RADICAL PRIESTS, AND FIFTY ASSORTED DRAFT DODGERS.

IN RETURN, THE U.S. WILL RECEIVE FIVE POETS, TWO BALLET DANCERS, AND A NOBEL PRIZE LAUREATE.

HEY, HONEY! YOU'RE NEW AROUND HERE! WHAT'S YER NAME?

ZONKER HARRIS.

MINE'S ALICE.. ALICE P. SCHWARTZMAN. I'M A GARMENT WORKER... AND A REGULAR!

'SIDE FROM THAT, I'M JUST AN AGIN' LADY... AS WORN OUT AND RAGGEDY AS AN OL' POT HOLDER... SIGH! GIMME A BEER..

MAY I SEE YOUR I.D., PLEASE, MISS?

HEE, HEE!.. BLESS YOU, DARLIN'!

BONKER. I WANNA TELL YOU A STRANGE, TRUE STORY. ONCE THERE WAS A PRETTY LITTLE GIRL WITH SATIN BOWS IN HER HAIR AND DREAMS IN HER HEART...

BUT ONE DAY SHE GREW UP AND FOUND THAT LIFE WAS NOT THE HAPPINESS SHE HAD THOUGHT IT. IT WAS FILLED WITH DESPAIR AND 35 YEARS OF HARD, LONELY WORK.

AND... BONKER... BONKER?

YES, ALICE?

BONKER, THAT LITTLE GIRL WAS *ME*!

I GUESSED, ALICE.

HAVE YOU KNOWN ALICE LONG, HANK?

ALICE? OH, SURE. ALMOST 30 YEARS NOW...

I GOTTA LOT OF RESPECT FOR THAT GAL. SHE'S SMART, AND HAS REAL STYLE AND DIGNITY. YOU KNOW, I MIGHT EVEN LIKE HER BETTER NOW THAN I DID 30 YEARS AGO!

WHY? WHAT WAS SHE LIKE THEN?

SHE WAS A TEASIN' LITTLE TART.

COME AGAIN?

BUILT, TOO.

YOU GUYS BOUGHT ME A BIRTHDAY PRESENT? WHAT IS IT?

WELL OPEN IT UP AND SEE, ALICE!

A BOWLING BALL!

YEP! THAT THERE IS A "PRINCESS TEN-PINS"— THE LIGHTWEIGHT MODEL FOR DAMES!

GOLLY,.. I'VE GOT TO BE THE LUCKIEST BARFLY THIS SIDE OF BROOKLYN..

AW, AIN'T NOTHIN' TOO GOOD FOR OUR ALICE'S BIRTHDAY.

SET 'EM UP, BONKER BABY!

RIGHT ON, YOUR GRACE!

LISSEN, MEN-FOLK, SEEIN' HOW THIS HERE'S MY BIRTH-DAY — WHICH YOU ALL KINDLY REMEMBERED — I WANNA TAKE THE FLOOR TO TELL A STORY, ABOUT ME GROWIN' UP IN NEW YORK..

WHEN I WAS ABOUT 16, I USED TO STAND OUTSIDE THE PLAZA HOTEL AT CHRISTMAS TIME TO WATCH THE DEBUTANTES ARRIVIN'! "HI, GLORIA!" I'D YELL. "HI, WENDY! HI, CONSUELA! HI, CHRISTINA!".. BUT THEY NEVER WAVED BACK..

YEARS LATER, I FINALLY FIGURED OUT THAT SOCIETY AND MONEY DON'T REALLY MEAN "CLASS" AT ALL! THE FOLKS HERE ARE THE ONES WITH THE CLASS. — THEY GOT TIME FOR AN OL' LADY...

BRING ON THE VIOLINS!

HEE HEE!

THAT WAS BEAUTIFUL, ALICE.

HARRIS! PUT THAT JOINT OUT!

HARRIS, PUT IT OUT OR YOU'RE OFF THE TEAM! YOU'RE HAVING A BAD EFFECT ON THE REST OF THE GUYS!

IT'S TRUE! ZONKER'S SETTING A TERRIBLE EXAMPLE! I'M.. I'M ABOUT TO SUCCUMB!

ME, TOO! I CAN'T TAKE THE PEER-GROUP PRESSURE ANY LONGER!

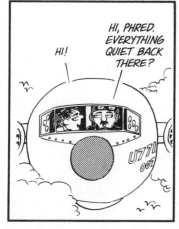

IV/Tripping Down the Hangout Route

Our passion for instant nostalgia would seem inexhaustible and cunning, especially in times of crisis. Taking two widely disparate cases in point, we have the Watergate Many reuning over Mrs. Dean's onion dip and serenading themselves as "Richard Nixon's Secret Tapes Club Band," while that other crisis, the one affecting everybody's gas tank, finds Mark Slackmeyer dusting off his revolutionary regalia preparatory to coaching some discontent truckers in the art of confrontation. And at the eyes of the two storms, things are positively medieval—as Fort Nixon digs in for the good of future Presidents, and the Energy Czar calls for hot wax and signet ring to allocate an extra five gallons for a mother's son forced to live two months at a turnpike Hot Shoppe. But *Time* marches on—indeed, it sends a totally credulous reporter to interview Zonker on "The New Hedonism"—and a few souls work to nobler purposes, though Joanie finds the road to law school more than a little rocky. But there are many ways to stonewall.

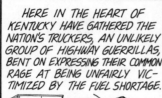

I'M REALLY GONNA BE ON T.V., HUH?

YEAH, IF WE CAN GET THIS FILMED IN TIME. NOW DON'T SAY ANYTHING WHILE I DO THE LEAD-IN, OKAY?

HERE IN THE HEART OF KENTUCKY HAVE GATHERED THE NATION'S TRUCKERS, AN UNLIKELY GROUP OF HIGHWAY GUERRILLAS, BENT ON EXPRESSING THEIR COMMON RAGE AT BEING UNFAIRLY VICTIMIZED BY THE FUEL SHORTAGE.

J.W. SNEAD IS ONE SUCH DRIVER. FOR HIM, LIFE IS A BRUTAL, DUSTY ROAD, A STARK NIGHT CAFÉ, ENDLESS HOURS OF ANGUISH BEHIND THE WHEEL OF A RIG HE MUST DRIVE RELENTLESSLY TO FEED A FAMILY WHO KNOWS ONLY..

AW, HELL, IT'S NOT THAT BAD!

CUT..

ANYWAY, I WOULDN'T WORRY ABOUT IT— THE ODDS ARE THAT THEY WON'T EVEN HAVE GAS... THIS ISN'T 1968, YOU KNOW..

WHAT IF WE GET HAULED IN?...

NO PROBLEM. THERE'S A BONDSMAN ALREADY DOWN THERE..

NOW, REMEMBER, WHEN THE ACTION STARTS, JUST TRY TO RELAX, HANG LOOSE. A GOOD DEMONSTRATION SHOULD ALWAYS BE THOUGHTFULLY PLANNED, BUT ORGANICALLY EXECUTED! ANY LAST QUESTIONS?

YEAH. DO WE HAFTA TAKE MARIJUANA OR SOMETHIN' BEFORE?

NO, THAT WON'T BE NECESSARY.

NO! NO! NO! STAND FIRM! LINK ARMS! DON'T LET THAT TRUCK THROUGH!... NO! NO! REGROUP!

;SIGH!;

PRETTY DISORGANIZED, HUH?

YOU SAID IT! THESE POOR GUYS ARE SUCH RANK AMATEURS!

NOT LIKE THE OLD DAYS, EH, LONG-HAIR..?

NO WAY, OFFICER..

WHAT A BOMB! A FIFTEEN MINUTE PROTEST!

YOU MUSTN'T BLAME YOURSELF. THE TRUCKERS ARE NEW AT CIVIL DISOBEDIENCE.

I SUPPOSE YOU'RE RIGHT, BUT WHERE DOES THAT LEAVE THEM?

FRANKLY, I THINK YOUR ONLY REAL CHOICE IS TO GO TO WASHINGTON!

YOU MEAN... YOU MEAN... .. TO SEE..

YES.. YES..

THE CZAR HIMSELF?!

WHY, I HEAR HE'S VERY NICE!

To: Photo Editor
From: Roland Burton Hedley, Jr.

This is Zonker Harris, 19, member of Walden.

Walden Commune—located about ½ mile from campus..

This is the backyard marijuana plant, which Zonker claims yields the highest grade grass in New England!

ROLAND, THAT'S A *LILAC* BUSH!

IT IS?..

ROLAND, I CAN'T BELIEVE THAT MOST COLLEGE STUDENTS HAVE BECOME SO *DECADENT!* ARE YOU *SURE* YOU VERIFIED THIS TREND ACROSS THE COUNTRY?

NO. I DIDN'T HAVE TO.

YOU DIDN'T *HAVE* TO?! WHAT DO YOU *MEAN?!*

THE STUDENTS I TALKED TO GAVE ME THEIR *WORD* OF HONOR THAT THEY REPRESENTED A NATIONAL TREND.

ROLAND, WHAT DID YOU COVER AT THE SAIGON BUREAU?

SPORTS.

CLACKITY! CLAK! *CLACKITY!* CLACK

TIME

The New Hedonism

EXTRA! LATEST STUDENT MOOD!

Chicago Tri on sale here

"SEX! SEX AND PEYOTE!" HE REPLIED.

I'M IN *BIG* TROUBLE..

MAN, I NEVER *DREAMED* HE'D PRINT ALL THAT STUFF! IT'S ABSOLUTELY *INCREDIBLE!*

ROLAND BURTON HEDLEY, JR. REALLY TAKES THE *PRIZE,* YOU KNOW THAT?! WE COULD HAVE TOLD HIM WE WERE *EXPATRIATED ZULUS* AND HE WOULD HAVE BELIEVED US!

AW, C'MON, DON'T WORRY ABOUT IT, ZONK — YOU'RE GONNA BE THE NEW DARLING OF "TIME'S" READER-SHIP!

RIGHT, ZONK! YOU'LL BE *FAMOUS!* YOU'LL BE NATIONALLY *KNOWN!*

TERRIFIC. A NATIONALLY KNOWN PERVERT..

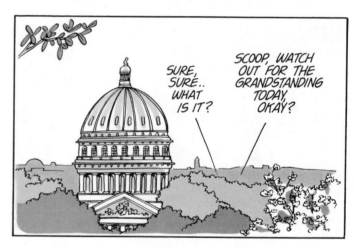

WELL.. I DUNNO, SIR... WITH ALL DUE RESPECT, I THINK WE'RE RUNNING OUT OF PLACES YOU'RE WELCOME TO SPEAK...

WELL, CHECK YOUR LIST AGAIN! IT'S CRUCIAL THAT WE MOVE FORWARD IN BREAKING THE BACK OF MY CREDIBILITY GAP!

WELL.. HERE'S ONE, MR. PRESIDENT— FRITTERS, ALABAMA! POPULATION 1,635. ALL WHITE, 95% OF WORK FORCE WORKING ON GOVERNMENT CONTRACTS!

WHY, IT'S PERFECT, SIR!

"FRITTERS, ALABAMA"?

REPEATING THE TOP STORY. TOMORROW THE PRESIDENT WILL BE FLYING TO FRITTERS, ALABAMA, TO DELIVER A MAJOR SPEECH!

FRITTERS, ALABAMA! CAN YOU BELIEVE IT?! WHAT A JOKE! HA, HA, HEE!

LESS'N, OF COURSE, Y'ALL HAPPIN TO LIVE THERE.

WASHINGTON POST!? WHERE'D YOU GET THAT PAPER, BOY?!

LIBRARY, POP... TEACHER SAYS IF THE PRESIDENT'S COMIN' TO FRITTERS, WE OUGHTA READ UP ON THE BIG PROBLEM HE'S HAVIN' IN WASHINGTON!

HOGWASH, BOY! YOU DON'T NEED A FANCY PAPER LIKE THAT TO KNOW WHAT'S GOIN' ON. DO YOU THINK THE PRESIDENT EVER READS PAPERS LIKE THAT?! YOU KIN BET YOUR BOOTS HE DON'T!

TEACHER SAYS THAT'S PART OF THE PROBLEM.

YOU SASSIN' ME, BOY?!

THERE HE IS, POP!

YUP AND HE'S GETTIN' A MESS OF CHEERS! FOLKS HERE IN FRITTERS BELIEVE IN AMERICA!

POP, YOU MEAN BELIEVIN' IN AMERICA IS THE SAME THANG AS BELIEVIN' IN PRESIDENT NIXON?

OF COURSE! IT STANDS TO REASON, DON'T IT?

HOW YA FIGURE, POP?

SHUT UP AND WAVE YOUR FLAG, BOY!

MR. PRESIDENT, I'M BEGINNING TO THINK PERHAPS IT MIGHT BE BETTER IF WE WERE MORE COMPLIANT IN PROVIDING MATERIALS TO THE HOUSE COMMITTEE...

JIM! HOW CAN YOU SUGGEST THAT?! I THOUGHT YOU WERE INTERESTED IN *PROTECTING* THE PRESIDENCY!

WELL, I STILL AM, SIR, BUT..

JIM, IT IS NOT *ME* I'M THINKING OF. IT'S A MATTER OF SETTING PRECEDENT! WHAT ABOUT *FUTURE PRESIDENTS?!*

OH, I IMAGINE THEY'LL MUDDLE THROUGH SOMEHOW, SIR..

DON'T BE CUTE, JIM.

BERKELEY PUT YOU ON THEIR WAITING LIST? WHAT DOES *THAT* MEAN?

IT MEANS I MIGHT GET IN IF SOME OF THOSE WHO WERE ACCEPTED TURN DOWN THE SCHOOL.

YOU MEAN YOU'RE ONLY OFFERED A SPOT IF SOMEONE ELSE DOESN'T WANT IT?

WELL, YES, THAT'S RIGHT.

DOESN'T THAT KIND OF CHEAPEN IT?

YOU'RE ON *ANOTHER* WAITING LIST?..

YUP. GEORGETOWN UNIVERSITY.

HOW MANY'S THAT?

WITH B.U. AND HARVARD, THAT MAKES *FOUR!* *NO* ACCEPTANCES. MY CHANCES OF MOVING AWAY TO LAW SCHOOL LOOK PRETTY BLEAK NOW..

I'M CRUSHED.

≀SIGH≀ SOME LEGAL EAGLE..

MS. CAUCUS, IS BEING ON A WAITING LIST REALLY SUCH A BAD THING?

OH, YES! IT'S ALMOST AS BAD AS BEING REJECTED!

YOU SEE, THE ANXIETY BUILDS UP AND UP, AND THE PRESSURE BECOMES UNBEARABLE AS YOU WAIT DAY AFTER DAY AFTER DAY, WONDERING IF YOU HAVE ANY FUTURE, ANY CAREER, ANYTHING TO LIVE FOR!

FORTUNATELY, SOME WOMEN HAVE WHAT IT TAKES TO PERSEVERE, TO HANG ON, TO HOLD THEIR HEADS HIGH NO MATTER WHAT THE OUTCOME!! MS. CAUCUS IS *ONE SUCH WOMAN!*

YEA!!

YOU GOTTA BELIEVE!

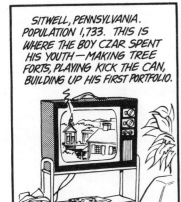

MS. ISABELLE GREBBLE. YOU WERE THE MONEY CZAR'S SECOND-GRADE TEACHER. WHAT CAN YOU TELL US ABOUT HIM?

WELL, I'LL NEVER FORGET HOW MUCH THE LITTLE TYKE USED TO LOVE MONEY! RIGHT FROM THE DAY HE SET UP HIS FIRST BUSINESS, A LEMONADE STAND!

HEE, HEE! I REMEMBER THE LEMONADE USED TO COST HIM 25¢... ONE DAY, AFTER THREE HOURS OF SELLING, HE CAME RUNNING IN WITH 12¢ AND YELLED, "LOOK, MISS GREBBLE, I MADE A NET PROFIT OF 85%!"

HE WAS WRONG, OF COURSE, BUT IT WAS SO ADORABLE!

THE COLLEGE YEARS. THE UBIQUITOUS CZAR-TO-BE WAS A STANDOUT! AN ECONOMICS MAJOR, CLASS TREASURER, AND RESPECTED FRATERNITY MAN.

HIS COLLEGE SWEETHEART, LAURA, NOW MRS. EDDIE BAJOLSKI, REMEMBERS...

THE CZAR REALLY WAS THE MOST MARVELOUS MAN...

HE ALWAYS LOOKED LIKE A MILLION DOLLARS, HE DRESSED TO KILL, AND HE COULD DANCE LIKE ASTAIRE. I ALMOST MARRIED HIM, BUT THEN I... I MET EDDIE.

I'VE NEVER LOOKED BACK.

HEE, HEE!

WALL STREET. NEW YORK'S YELLOW BRICK ROAD. THE PLACE WHERE A THOUSAND DREAMS ARE REALIZED OR SHATTERED. IT WAS HERE THE YOUNG CZAR FIRST CAME TO SEEK HIS FORTUNE.

BROKERS, INDUSTRIALISTS, BANKERS, MONEY MAGNATES OF ALL KINDS — THESE ARE BILL SIMON'S PEOPLE. THESE ARE THE PEOPLE WHO WATCHED AS HE COOLLY WENT ABOUT MAKING HIS FIRST MILLION.

ALBIE ROBERTS, A FELLOW BROKER IN THE CZAR'S OLD FIRM.

THE GUY WAS A BUM. HE'D SELL HIS OWN CHILDREN IF THE MARKET WERE RIGHT.

YES, IT'S A TOUGH SCENE, WALL STREET..

HOW LONG BILL SIMON PLANS TO STAY ON AT TREASURY IS ANYONE'S GUESS. BUT IN THE MEANTIME, WASHINGTON HAS A NEW STAR.

CZAR. THE MAN AND THE MONEY.

I'M JOHN CHANCELLOR. GOOD NIGHT.

WOOF!

HONEY, HOW COME SHE ISN'T GETTING ALPO?!

JOANIE, BEFORE I HELP YOU WITH THE APARTMENT HUNTING, I GOTTA GO CHECK IN WITH MY UNCLE DUKE.

I DIDN'T KNOW YOU HAD AN UNCLE DUKE.

WELL, HE'S NOT REALLY MY UNCLE—HE'S AN OLD FAMILY FRIEND. HE WRITES FOR "ROLLING STONE" MAGAZINE.

REALLY? WHAT'S HE LIKE?

QUITE NICE, BUT A LITTLE STRANGE—HE'S INCREDIBLY RECKLESS WITH DRUGS. PERIODICALLY, MOM HAS TO CALL THE POLICE AND HAVE HIM BUSTED. YOU KNOW, TO COOL HIM OFF.

HE DOESN'T MIND?

HECK, NO! IN CALIFORNIA, THAT'S WHAT FRIENDS ARE FOR!

I GUESS I BETTER CHECK ON THE SITUATION AT THE OFFICE BEFORE I GO OVER TO SEE UNCLE DUKE..

THE SITUATION?

YEAH—LATELY HE'S BEEN EXPERIMENTING WITH SOME BIZARRE SOUTH AMERICAN HALLUCINOGENS, SO A LOT OF THE TIME HE'S COMATOSE...

HELLO, I'M TRYING TO REACH DUKE—I WONDER IF YOU COULD TELL ME IF HE'S CONSCIOUS... HE IS?.. HE'S FULLY CONSCIOUS? HEY, THAT'S GREAT! TELL HIM ZONKER IS COMING OVER TO VISIT, OKAY? THANKS!

WHAT A RELIEF!—HE'S..

YEAH, I HEARD.

UNCLE DUKE?

ZONKER! WHAT A SURPRISE! LONG TIME, HOMBRE!

WHAP!

YES, IT CERTAINLY HAS BEEN. WHAT ARE YOU DOING ON THE FLOOR, UNCLE DUKE?

KILLING BATS WITH MY RULER! REALLY BIG ONES, TOO!

WHAP!

BATS?

YEAH—WHENEVER I HAVE TOO MUCH TEQUILA AND COKE, I START TO SEE HUGE, HAIRY BATS!

SO TELL ME—HOW'S YOUR MOTHER?

WHAP!

WHATCHA WORKIN' ON NOW, UNCLE DUKE?

NOTHIN' SPECIAL. JUST SOME A-1, SUPERFINE GUERRILLA REPORTAGE!

SEE, I'VE BEEN UP FOR SIX STRAIGHT DAYS ON ALL SORTS OF GOODIES, SO I CAN'T QUITE RECALL WHAT IT IS I'M WRITING ABOUT. BUT YOU CAN BE SURE IT'S OUTRAGEOUSLY SATIRICAL.

I JUST WRITE WHATEVER POPS INTO MY PILL-CRAZED HEAD—I SCRIBBLE DOWN PART OF IT, DICTATE SOME OF IT, AND SEND THE REST IN BY CABLE! MY EDITORS ARE GREAT ABOUT IT—THEY'LL PRINT IT ALL!

YEAH, BUT DOES IT PLAY IN PEORIA?

OF COURSE NOT! THAT'S THE WHOLE POINT!

V/Brightening Up Our Tarnished Age

The crises break and the walls come down. Not only are the gates working again at the White House, but for this President even poolside isn't too chummy a milieu for meeting the press. And out at Berkeley, the new chumminess gets to Joanie, too, as she finds that having a right-on, law school roommate like Virginia means contending as well with her boyfriend, an improbable homebody named Clyde. If not all of the nation's wounds are healing—witness the lunchroom melee instigated by an eight-year-old participant of forced busing—things do seem to have settled down. And yet . . . Suppose we could get back to when it all started, or even imagine ourselves at Scot Sloan's publication party—with his cat Kent State, with the university president who remembers how it was, with all the gang playing their "best and brightest" roles. Have we come a long enough way to make sport of it all? Or should we wonder, with Mark and Mike, what happened to us?

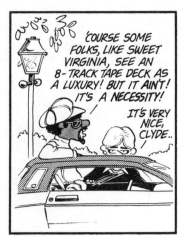

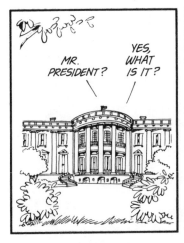

TORTS?.. NO, I DON'T WANT TO TALK ABOUT TORTS! WE JUST SPENT ALL MORNING TALKING ABOUT TORTS!

WOODROW, WHAT YOU'VE GOT TO REALIZE IS THAT THE WORLD DOESN'T BEGIN AND END WITH CASEBOOKS! THERE ARE MANY OTHER EQUALLY ACCEPTABLE WAYS OF LOOKING AT LIFE!

HMM..

YEAH, I SUPPOSE YOU COULD MAKE A CASE FOR THAT..

WELL, REALLY NOW, WOODROW, IT'S ONLY A MATTER OF CIVIL PROCEDURE!

TRUE—BUT ONLY AS FAR AS IT AFFECTS THE INCLUSION OF PARTIES NECESSARY FOR THE DISPOSITION!

HEY, PEOPLE! I'VE GOT A REALLY CRAZY, FAR-OUT, ZANY IDEA! LET'S SPEND PART OF LUNCH TALKING ABOUT SOMETHING OTHER THAN LAW!

FORGIVE ME. I LOST MY HEAD.

WHO IS THIS CHICK?

JOAN SOMEBODY.

Dear Mr. President,

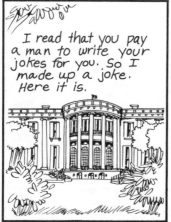

I read that you pay a man to write your jokes for you. So I made up a joke. Here it is.

You say, "I am a Ford, not a Lincoln, and Ford has a better idea."

Please pay me $10.00 for this joke. Your friend, Billy R.

WHERE DO YOU THINK YOU'RE GOING, YOUNG MAN?

I'M MOVIN' IN WITH VIRGINIA, POCATELLI.

BANG! BANG!

WELL, AS I UNDERSTAND IT, VIRGINIA DOESN'T WANT YOU TO MOVE IN!

HEY, POCATELLI— YOU GO MIND YOUR OWN BUSINESS, HEAR?

ZIP!

OH, HI, CLYDE— WHAT'S UP?

HELLO?.. GET ME THE BERKELEY POLICE!

UH..CAN I COME IN?.. QUICK?!

DEPENDS, LOVER— WHAT DO WE GOT HERE?

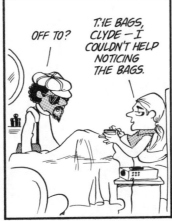

CLYDE, LOOK—HERE'S WHERE I'M AT: I HAPPEN TO LIKE YOU VERY MUCH, AND I PLACE A LOT OF VALUE ON OUR FRIENDSHIP. I ALSO THINK YOU'RE ONE OF THE SEXIER PEOPLE I'VE EVER MET..

BUT, ALL THAT NOTWITHSTANDING, I DON'T WANT TO GET MARRIED, I DON'T WANT TO LIVE WITH ANYONE—I JUST WANT ROOM TO GROW AND BREATHE. CAN'T YOU ACCEPT THAT?

≶SIGH≶..
YEAH.. YEAH, I GUESS I CAN DIG IT..

S'LONG AS YOU REALLY MEAN THE SEXY PART!

HEY, C'MON! YOU SLAY ME, LOVER.

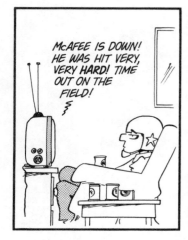

McAFEE IS DOWN! HE WAS HIT VERY, VERY HARD! TIME OUT ON THE FIELD!

THE DOCTORS ARE RUSHING OUT ON THE FIELD.. THEY'RE CHECKING HIM OUT... McAFEE'S BEING PUT ON THE STRETCHER!

ROG, WE JUST GOT A REPORT HERE FROM OUR MAN ON THE FIELD! IT SEEMS THAT McAFEE IS...UH.. ≶ DEAD.

YES, BUT WHAT A HAND HE'S GETTING THERE, JACK!

RIGHT! I'LL TELL YOU, ROGER—THESE ARE SOME KINDA FOOTBALL ≶ FANS!

AS PART OF NBC'S CONTINUING COVERAGE OF THE MARIJUANA CRISIS, TODAY WE INTERVIEW DR. R.G. TULANE, WHO RECENTLY LINKED THE USAGE OF MARIJUANA TO BRAIN DAMAGE!

DOCTOR, WE UNDER-STAND THAT HEAVY EXPOSURE TO MARI-JUANA HAS CAUSED SOME INSIDIOUS EFFECTS IN YOUR RHESUS MONKEYS!

THAT IS CORRECT...

MY MONKEYS WERE GIVEN A CONTROLLED DAILY DOSAGE. AFTER ONLY TWO WEEKS, INTENSIVE INTER-VIEWS WERE CONDUCTED WITH EACH OF THEM.

AND?..

THEY WERE ALL TOTALLY INCOHERENT.

UH-OH..

HEY, REV— WHAT A NICE SURPRISE! WHAT BRINGS YOU OUT HERE?

ZONKER, IT'S MY NOVEL— IT'S FINALLY BEEN ACCEPTED FOR PUBLI-CATION!

THEY SAY THEY LOVE IT! THEY SAY I'M GOING TO BE FAMOUS, A STAR! I'M BEING SENT ON A 30-CITY TOUR— TALK SHOWS, AUTO-GRAPH PARTIES, THE WORKS!

HEY, THAT'S GREAT, SCOTTY!

THAT'S WHY I CAME OUT HERE, ZONK! I HAD TO GET OUT OF THE CITY, TO GET IN TOUCH WITH MYSELF BEFORE IT ALL BEGINS!

OH... WELL, YOU CAN USE MIKE'S ROOM IF YOU WANT..

THANKS, ZONK. I APPRECIATE IT!

SO WHAT'S THIS NEW BLOCKBUSTER OF YOURS ABOUT, REV?

WELL, IT TRACES THE GROWTH OF A YOUNG PHILOSOPHY STUDENT WHO GETS INVOLVED IN THE BERKELEY FREE-SPEECH MOVEMENT, THEN MOVES ON TO A BUDDHIST COMMUNE IN MICHIGAN..

MORE! MORE!

LATER, HE IS ARRESTED FOR CONSPIRACY IN CHICAGO, BUT ESCAPES TO BECOME A MEDIC AT WOODSTOCK. FINALLY, FREAKED OUT OVER THE WAR, AND WIRED ON SIX TABS OF ACID, HE DRIVES HIS V.W. CAMPER OVER A CLIFF AT MALIBU!

IT'S SORT OF ABOUT THE SIXTIES.

YEAH, MAN, I BEEN THERE..

MICHAEL! DID YOU HEAR ABOUT THE GOOD REVEREND'S NOVEL?!

YOU BET! I JUST SAW HIM THIS MORNING. HE DROPPED BY WALDEN WITH A PHOTOGRAPHER!

WITH A PHOTOGRAPHER? WHAT FOR?

HE WANTS TO BORROW OUR SCENERY FOR A BACK JACKET PHOTO..

HOW'S THIS?

CLICK! GOOD! CLICK! GOOD! OKAY, NOW LET'S SEE SOME TEETH!

WHATCHA DOING NOW, W.S.?

WRITING MY BIO. FOR THE JACKET FLAP...

TAP! TAP! TAP!

W.S. Sloan, Jr., is a dedicated activist of long standing. He was once described by "Look" magazine as "the fighting young priest who makes a difference."

TAP! TAP! TAP!

Mr. Sloan resides in New England. He lives alone with his faithful Irish setter, Unconditional Amnesty.

TAP! TAP! TAP!

DON'T FORGET OL' KENT STATE..

..and his cat, Kent State.

TAP! TAP! TAP!

ZONKER! YOU'RE ALL DRESSED UP!

YUP! I'M OFF TO SCOT'S PUBLICATION PARTY! HE'S HAVING A SORT OF SIXTIES REVIVAL COSTUME BALL!

SIXTIES REVIVAL?

YOU KNOW—STROBE LIGHTS, OPPRESSIVELY LOUD MUSIC, LOTS OF PSYCHEDELICS—THAT SORT OF THING!

SOUNDS LIKE FUN! WHAT'S THAT YOU GOT ON—SORT OF GYPSY GARB?

NOPE. IT'S MY SICK, TWISTED, NEO-FASCIST DRUG-FIEND DISGUISE.

OH. WELL, YOU LOOK JUST GREAT!

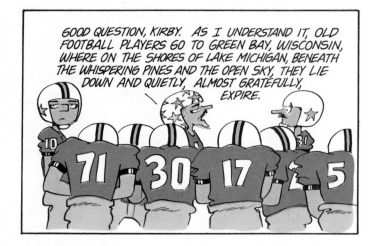

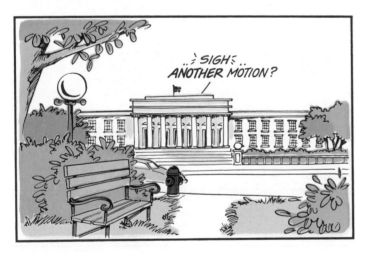

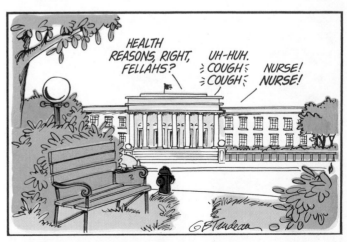

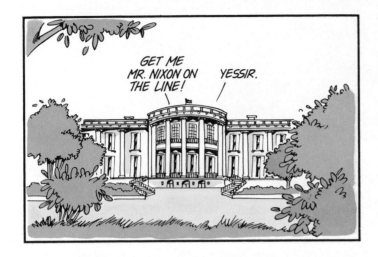

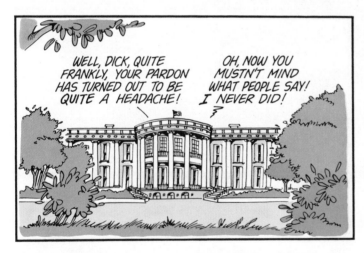

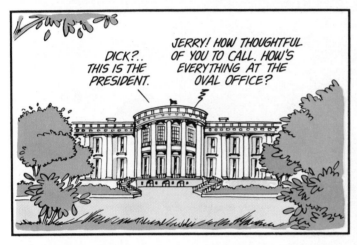

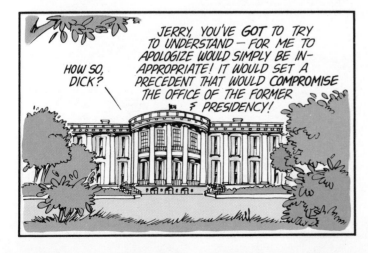